MW01386166

Moon Rising

An Eclectic Collection of Works

Ann Edall-Robson

Suite 300 - 990 Fort St
Victoria, BC, Canada, V8V 3K2
www.friesenpress.com

ISBN
978-1-4602-5680-0 (Hardcover)
978-1-4602-5681-7 (Paperback)
978-1-4602-5682-4 (eBook)

1. Literary Collections, General

Distributed to the trade by The Ingram Book Company

To my daughters Dana and Tanis who are inspirations to life itself.

To Steve; my confidant, my rock, my constant support.
You are the best, my man.

Prepare the day
A vision at dawn
Yours to hold
Inimitable unto itself
To keep always

Ann Edall-Robson

"Always keep a deck of cards with you when you are headed into the bush alone. If you get lost, there is a pretty good chance someone will come along and tell you to put the red six on the black seven."

I. K. (Bud) Edall

Ann Edall-Robson has invited us to share a bit about her world in *Moon Rising* . . . A series of intimate vignettes; her thoughtful arrangement of words and images encourages us to fondly consider certain perspectives that may seem quite routine to some. She reminds us to tap into our own memories and leads us back to that safe, comfortable place as we reminisce about the 'usual'. But everything is celebrated by Ann! Her descriptive observations become the magic that transforms these normal occurrences into something 'special'. And we are that much richer for recognizing the wondrous world that Ann has returned us to . . . a reward for taking the time to immerse ourselves in life's bounties!

Debbie Jo Webster
Chimney Rock Bed and Breakfast
'Ma' Dame of Dames on the Range

Moon Rising has a way of transporting the reader to a place where memories live, and where the past isn't so distant. The poetry and prose are skillfully paired by the Author herself. It is a wonderful collection.

Lori Stafford

In *Moon Rising*, Ann Edall-Robson skillfully shares her poetry, prose and photographs. This collection of work enables the reader to experience the richness of rural life. Her work covers a wide range of emotions. The nostalgia had me longing for a life I'd never known. Writing from different points of view gave me unexpected insight. The vivid imagery used pulled me into her stories as if I were experiencing them alongside of her. This is a book that you will enjoy reading and re-reading.

Tandy Balson
Author - *Inspirations From The Everyday*

Author's Note

I write what I see in my mind's eye, whatever inspires me; a sunset, a memory, a lesson learned or life itself. *Moon Rising* is an anthology of adventures, places, and times – writings gathered from the last forty-five years, released from the memory bank and shared from the heart.

Table of Contents

HOMECOMING

The gravel road is a welcoming sight. The familiar landmarks let me know I am not far from where I want to be; a comfort zone that encourages a smile on my face. It gets bigger as I sing along to old favourites coming through the airwaves. It has been a while since I have travelled these roads. The anticipation is bouncing through my mind and body as I navigate the ruts and pot-holes. Two more cattle guards to cross and it will be time to turn off and head northwest for a few miles through the poplars to the place I see in my mind; the open expanse of meadows and ponds where the foothills dance with colour as they make their way to the majestic mountains . . . so close and yet so far away. A beautiful homecoming is always there, at the end of the gravel road.

A CHILD'S EYES

Through the eyes of the child,
they could be seen.
Huge on the horizon,
moving towards the open field.
Not a thing to stop
their charge forward.
Anticipation of their arrival
visible in the child's face.
No fear, only calm prevailed
in the eyes of one so small.
Stories of this day
have formulated.
How they came
and how they hovered.
How they moved on
in the wind.

Arriving as one,
leaving as another.
Some gathering together,
others coming alone.
No two the same,
both pleasing and foreboding.
To the trained eye
of a small child who saw them all.
They will come back another day
limited only to the imagination.
The child will be waiting
to welcome the shapes in the clouds once again.

LOVE IN A BLENDER

I wonder what it is that makes us think we are in love with someone. What makes in-love and loving so different? And there is a difference.

Yes, different because we love in so many different ways. Think about how we love our pets and childhood stuffed animals; the feeling of love for our parents and siblings. I call this family love. No matter where you are in life you can always take it with you.

Friendship hovers on the edge of its own meaning of love and being a part of family love. Love for friends is a nourishing growth that creates a bond between people, which is unforgettable and is kept with you forever.

Finally, we get to the being-in-love kind of love. A feeling that throws all of the emotions into a blender, and goes through the pulse, blend, whip, and puree cycles to end up as part of a recipe. It can be indescribable when shared with a person who believes that life is aligned as it should be. A life and time that have no beginning or end when you are with someone you are in love with.

PUZZLE

A jigsaw puzzle,
like our lives
comes with many pieces
that fit together.

Once all of the bits
are found
and the last one
is put in place,

There is a sense
of pride and fulfillment
knowing the many shapes
have become one.

I am grateful
that you are the
last piece
to the puzzle.

SPIRITS OF THE ROAD HOUSE

. . . A feeling of déjà vu creeps into the conscious thoughts. Goose bumps form on the arms and the hair is prickling at the base of the neck. This is the first visit to this old dwelling. It feels comfortable. The floor plan can be visualized in the mind without entering the building. There's a familiarity of what would be behind each door without opening them . . .

Stepping inside this old world, there is a presence of people, yet there is not a person in sight. They are busy. They are friendly. They nod and smile. They move from inside to out and back again. Some are sitting on the bench outside the door enjoying the day as they wait. Still others take a beverage or a meal at the long table inside.

The big fireplace at the end of the kitchen is a welcoming feature. Stacks of wood are nearby, waiting for those cold mornings and winter days when they will be used to heat the room. On the wood stove there is food simmering and the fire crackles within. The floor creaks as a door opens, showing off a sitting area where the ladies wait in comfort – some reading, some doing needlework, others visiting.

Through the kitchen window there is the view of the big barn and corrals. In anticipation of the arrival of the next stagecoach, there are men in the pens throwing hay into the mangers, and the gate to the pasture and creek beyond has been opened. Six fresh horses are being readied with harnesses. It won't be long until the stage arrives and they will be put to work on the next leg of the journey. They too will be changed out when they reach then next road house some twenty miles away.

The hustle and bustle will subside once the stage leaves and the passengers that arrived go on their way. For the next week or so, it will be the day-to-day chores and preparations for the next arrival, which will keep those that live here busy.

. . . The old buildings have seen much in their time. They hold the spirits of those that came to this land and their walls have many stories to share. Some were a residence for a lifetime and others were only a stopover for a few hours before the people moved on . . .

LOVERS

A few months of happiness

Broken off like a twig in a storm

Untouchable unforgettable

Meeting occasionally

Speaking, even touching

Feelings penetrated too deep

The lonely silence times

Wander to the memories

The tenderness, the hurt

Once lovers

BUD PUDDLES

The Bud Puddles, yes, Bud Puddles, carry on year after year. We have no control as to how many there will be or what time of year they will appear; spring thaw brings out copious amounts of them and rain leaves them everywhere. Hot weather tends to make them shrivel and disappear while cold weather may make them into a completely different life form.

It must be spring, there are Bud Puddles everywhere. There are big ones, little ones, and ones that are continually on the move. They are here at the start of the day and quite often gone by early afternoon. They linger into the evening and get crusty around the edges as they freeze overnight. Children of all ages run through them and jump into them.

Bud had radar ability to make the parking of his vehicle an event; one that ended in the passenger door of said vehicle opening directly into the middle of a puddle. It is most certain this man got quite a kick out of the reaction he got from his passengers as they stepped out of the vehicle, oblivious to the waiting water. The unsuspecting were unaware of the position they were going to be in until it was too late and they were ankle deep in the freezing remnants of spring thaw.

All who rode in the passenger seat of Bud's vehicle were potential victims. Even after an inaugural dip in a puddle, it was a continual game of intrigue as to whether it would happen again. Or was it just an oversight on the driver's (Bud's) part? One never knew, until the next time.

FALL

Silence
except the sound of birds
and the creek.

Smatterings
of fluffy clouds draw the eyes
to the distant horizon.

Colours
in the willows along the creek
show signs of the changing season.

Leaves
nipped by frost are yellow and red
mixed into the hues of green.

Coniferous
on the ridge are a dark frame
for the tracts of poplar.

Creating
a peaceful retreat
for all who go there.

Fall
definitely has arrived
in the valley.

MORNING PALETTE

I sit waiting patiently as the diamond-studded sky fades to the early morning light. The smell of freshly brewed coffee pulls me away from my theatre. But only for as long as it takes to fill my cup and return to the window.

The soft yellow halo of the sun is all that is visible behind the silhouette of trees on the ridge. Like an explosion, vibrant streaks of pink, orange, and red shatter what's left of the night sky. A spectacular palette of hues mingles together on the snowy mountains. How quickly the colours change in their effort to welcome the day.

LIVESTOCK AT LARGE

Understanding why bovines do what bovines do can make a trip on a country road that much more enjoyable. They think for themselves, do not like to be rushed, and will make you shake your head in wonder! Slow down, be patient, and they will have you on your way in no time.

Next time you are travelling through open-range country:

> Pay close attention to the small herds of cattle that you might encounter.

> Granted, you should be slowed down to a crawl.

> As you progress forward, notice the first cow.

> It will not be making a move other than to lift its head and bawl as you go by.

> The second, third, and maybe even the fourth will do the same.

Creeping along, you are now nearing the end of the herd.

Soon you will be leaving the bovines behind.

This is when you really need to be on full alert, because that is when THIS will undoubtedly happen:

Just when you thought you were going to be on your way,

One will step out onto the road in front of your vehicle.

It will look past you and bawl loudly.

Since you are at a full stop, check the view behind you.

All of the other bovines who mooed as you went by them

Are now standing on the road looking in your direction.

You are boxed in with no place to go.

Pause here to enjoy the drama, this won't take long.

They are just letting you know who is boss in their country.

It must be a rule somewhere that the livestock you encounter in your travels are on a mission. They slow you down to help you enjoy the scenery and life in the country. After a few minutes of inconvenience in your travel plans, they will wander off to the side of the road to let you continue on your journey.

STANDING ALONE

Standing alone
Naked and cold
The memory of warmth from the sun
On outstretched limbs

Was it yesterday?
Or this morning?

The breeze causes shivers
There is a whisper
But no words
A rustling of activity

Then silence
It's getting colder

Barely any movement
Not long and sleep will take over
Ending this part of the cycle
Life will carry on

It always does
When the cold is gone

And sun and the rain
Welcome spring and life
To the outstretched arms
Of the cottonwood trees

I WISH YOU

I wish you dreams that soothe your soul.

I wish you dreams that give you visions.

I wish you dreams that are restful.

I wish you dreams that are tender and loving.

I wish you dreams that make you smile.

I wish you dreams that are of me.

A REFLECTION ON FIFTY

Fifty opens the door to the next half-century of life. When you say **Fifty** it is not an age unless you let it be. It doesn't matter how you look at it, if you have had your **fiftieth** birthday, the next day you ARE technically over **fifty,** so keep the following in mind as you journey forward . . .

Fifty gives you shock factor. Telling your age shocks the heck out of people. Acting your age shocks you.

Fifty increases your worth. This number in some circles would be considered a collectable bordering on antique.

Fifty lets you say 'NO' easier. You might not mean it, but it feels good just to say it and not have anyone question your words.

Fifty provides excellent excuse material.

> I CAN'T do that, what will people think of someone my age trying that? – This is a good place to remember the shock factor.
>
> I CAN do that because I am over **fifty.** – This too is reminiscent of the shock factor.
>
> I DID that?? Must be the age. – Shock factor strikes again!

Fifty is the payback chapter in life, letting you openly embarrass the children and they chalk it up to your age rather than, you really did mean to do it.

Fifty provides you with feathers. Now is the time to spread your wings. It is a known fact from quite a few; life CAN be nifty after **fifty.**

Fifty gives you two twenty-fives' of experience to take the best and worst of each and make the next twenty-five into the time of your life.

Fifty is just a number. Let it be what it is and it will let you be who you are . . . simply the best!!!

UP-SIDE-DOWN?

An interesting bit of history
Stood fast along the hill

Held in place with barbed wire
Quiet and oh-so-still

Lending itself to the ambiance
With the creek wandering below

For decades it has done its job
Through the wind, the rain, and snow

Its cap not flat as we would think
An oddity to the eye

Its pointed end not sunk in the dirt
But staring up at the sky

There is no mirth to the reasoning
And it's completely honour-bound

If it rots off at the bottom
Just drive the top into the ground

RASPBERRY PATCH

. . . It has been a year since the last visit to Grandma's. The promise of rasp-
berries is etched in the mind of the child standing at the edge of the garden.
As she stands there, patient beyond her years, little hands are stuffed inside
pants pockets; she's waiting and watching for permission to go to the secret
spot amongst the thorny canes . . .

Wandering between the towering raspberry canes, every so often
stopping to pluck a fat berry that had been left behind by the adults
who had earlier filled buckets with the sweet, juicy fruit. Bending
closer to the garden floor to see if she could find any other strays
left behind is when she saw the opening between the canes – a dark
hole just big enough for her little-girl body to crawl through. It wasn't
scary. She could see the light shining through the fence on the other
side of the garden. On her hands and knees she ventured into this
unknown land.

It was when she was completely through the opening into her
secret hide-away that she saw them. They were clustered together
and nodding gently in the breeze with the sunlight filtering through

the leaves to illuminate their luscious hues of red. Reaching up, she gently tugged at the treasures hanging there. Easily they dropped into her tiny hand, perfect in shape and almost filling the little girl's palm. How could they have been left behind? Should she run to the house and announce her find? No, this would be her secret garden place.

And so, there she sat on that warm summer day, nestled under the raspberry canes, eating the fruit that no one else knew about; a small girl in her secret garden, dreaming of things to come.

. . . *In her garden paradise, the grown woman reminisces of a time when she was three. Back to the first time she had gone to the berry patch without an adult in tow – to the day she had discovered the hide-away in the raspberry patch . . .*

BUTTON

She needs some time
To find herself
The carefree girl
From days gone by

The quiet one
With a gentle soul
That loved to play
And dance all night

A venturous spirit
Her hair blowing free
Racing across fields
On her chestnut mare

The blue-eyed girl
With the long, dark hair
And tiny button nose
Where did she go?

PUDDLES

Age is a state of mind. Some days when I get to the edge of a puddle, I jump into it; making a splash, getting soaked, and laughing at my silly antics. Then there are the days I skirt the puddle, thinking I would like to jump through it, and don't. That is the grown-up in me that is supposed to know better.

There are days I wish I had three sets of feet . . . one for the puddles, one for the now, and one to reach out and tread on all there is yet to live and learn. Aging doesn't scare me; it intrigues me, knowing that anything I want to do is possible. If I don't like how things are in my life, I have the power to make change.

One thing I know for sure . . . there will always be puddles to make me smile.

THE SORREL MARE

Anyone who has owned or been around horses has been bucked off at least once. If you fell off you would never admit it . . . after all, a good rider doesn't fall off, they get bucked off.

Being bucked off unexpectedly can result in injury of some kind but has more often than not caused little more than wounded pride. You don't normally have a choice of venue when a horse decides to put you in the dirt. It comes when you least expect it and most certainly will add insult to injury! The upside is it comes with bragging rights!

You have the chance to tell your version of the event to whoever will listen. Zealous interpretations that could be construed as slightly exaggerated.

The sorrel mare was a prime example of a horse that liked to show how good she felt by throwing her heels to the sky and her nose to the ground, rarely letting fly when there was anyone on board. She would choose the most inopportune time and location to let you know she was feeling her oats, that's when all hell would break loose. She was just plain sneaky about when she would decide to perform. If she put her mind to dropping her head, a rider that was not paying attention could end up on the ground and walking home.

And that is how it came to be that a trip to the emergency room was needed to make sure there were no broken bones, but that the ego was kept somewhat intact. After all, a warning had been issued: "If you run that mare, watch that she doesn't buck you off!" But every teen knows that an adult is an unreliable source of advice so this caution went unheeded. When it came to the sorrel mare, a mile from the barn these words were to be proven . . .

On a gravel road surrounded by friends riding saddled horses, the challenge was issued as to who could get back to the barn first. The race was on. That was about the time that the teenager, who preferred to ride bareback, encountered an upside-down view of the mare's shoulder. Unceremonious, airborne antics ended with a solid landing on the gravel road. Seconds split in half could not have anticipated the quickness by which that mare deposited her rider elbow-first into a world of hurt, and headed to the barn.

The look of disgust on the sorrel's face when she was caught and brought back to carry the teenager home was priceless. It was almost as if she knew she was expected to fulfill her part of the old saying; "If you get bucked off, you get back on."

YOU

You let me sleep

You keep me awake

You give me happy

You give me tears

You let me rant

You give me support

You let me snuggle

You give me space

You took my call

You gave me life

FIRST

Time for me
Where did it go?
The priority has become too low
It is mine to have again
It's not so hard
All things else, step aside
Make time rules to abide
Break down the protective guard
Selfish, I think not
I am the one
Life around me will not come undone
When I put myself first

SNOWFLAKES

And there

In the silence of the night
You could see them coming
Not a sound they made
As they gathered

Slowly at first

As time passed
Their number grew
Joining together
Too many to count

Patiently

They wait in the fields
Under bushes
On paths
Silently, without a word

And again

When the time is right
They arrive once more
All different, but quite alike
Snowflakes

TEA SACK

A tea bag is as common as a cold to most. Yet there are still those who enjoy their cup of tea brewed the old-fashioned way. Start by rinsing the brewing pot with hot water. Add the loose tea of your choice. Pour boiling water over the dried leaves and let it steep until all is settled to the bottom of the pot. Give it a quick stir and let the leaves settle again. Pour into your favourite mug or cup using a tea strainer, or just pour and take your chances on how many leaves will end up in your cup. Alternatively, you can use a nifty little bag that is made to hold loose tea, a.k.a. a tea bag.

Now, for those that knew him, Ralph enjoyed a good cup of tea. Being brought up in the generation that steeped their tea, he was used to floaters and residue from the leaves being left in his cup. You can only imagine the consternation of this old-fashioned cowhand, when on a visit to town, he ordered tea at a restaurant and was brought a modern-day tea bag – something he had never been privy to viewing or using on the ranch. Not wanting to cause a scene, he quietly turned the tea bag over a few times, tore the bag apart, put the leaves into his mug and poured the boiling water over top. All the while, he was enlightening his tablemates with his colourful thoughts on why anyone would put tea in a sack!

Ralph is no longer with us, but the tale about how "Old T-Sack" got his nickname is still told. It's a story repeated out of respect and etched with humour about a good-natured man that was known to cowboy near the breaks of the Fraser River.

TREASURE

A world of treasure and surprise

Dreams to grasp

Nothing more than a wish

A thought

A passing whim

A word, a glance, a touch

Across a room, across miles

Anticipating nothing

Given with tenderness

Surprises to share

Found when least expected

Our love for each other

A world to treasure

HOPELESS ROMANTIC

It is the moon's fault. It makes people into hopeless romantics when it is full and just hanging out there for the world to enjoy.

Any full moon will do. On a clear night, there it is in all its glory; waiting for the time when couples can delight in its splendour. A walk in the dark, enjoyed from the deck, or in a parked car. Whatever . . . Where ever . . . Holding hands . . . Cuddling . . . Making the windows steamy . . . Anything and everything imaginable.

No matter how you look at it, it is romance. It is only who you share it with that makes it truly romantic. Enjoy your moon together.

WINTER

Drifting past the window
Slowly, lazily piling up
A bed full of fluff!

Beautiful, lovely shapes
Six sides – every one
Falling alone – becoming one.

Such clear silences
Making stunning scenes
A new world opens.

Crisp, white, and fresh
Lonely flakes falling
The still of winter is here.

THE WIRE AND POST CONTRAPTION

I can still see that old gate post with the rusted, makeshift latch hanging off to one side. Does it know how many arguments it started or how many cuss words were muttered because of its ability to seemingly not quite be long enough to fit over the gate?

Those were the days. The race to the truck to see who got to sit by the window only to find out that was the "chore seat"; the one place in the vehicle that was deemed by all who sat there as not only the open-the-gate seat, but the fight-with-the-gate-after, to-get-it-closed seat.

It wouldn't have been so bad if it was a wooden or metal gate, as they easily swing open and come back to their resting places without too much bother. It was the wire, or wire and post contraptions that had a mind of their own. Opening was relatively easy because stretching them out as they were opened seemed to be the answer, but it didn't always help. By the time the person in the "chore seat" walked back to the latch on the gate, the wire had somehow managed to get tangled with itself. It would twist and bend and would need to be pulled on, yanked, and stretched out, cajoled and muttered-at, so it would fit into the wire loop at the bottom of the gate post and then allow closure with the loop at the top. At the end of the day, with the stars and moon aligned, and the tongue held just right, the gate would settle where it was needed and everything would fall into place.

Driving away, watching the gate out the back window, all the while making a silent promise that next time the middle seat would be the answer so I wouldn't have to deal with THAT gate, again.

TEARS

Tears but for what?
Stream down soft cheeks
Silently they land
Each holds meaning

Of happiness
Raw emotion shown
Openly understood
Moulding life

Of sorrow
Like wet jewels
True feelings
Baring the soul

Of truth
Each person lives
Strength and honesty
To fulfill dreams

For what?
Life itself
Flows easily
Like a tear

NATURE'S PEOPLE

Alone, like daisies in a field
Hundreds more are near
Brushing lightly in movement
Never talking, never loving

Eyes stare out at nothing
Hoping someone will notice
Wanting to be picked
Tenderly taken in hand

Shyness is silence
Faces open to sunshine
Bringing life and beauty
No words are necessary

Nurture the life
Include the affection
Caring makes things live
People, too, need life

HE SNORED

He snored; and not just a light sound, but one that could rattle the windows. The sound was produced regardless of whether he laid on his back, his side, or his stomach.

On a particular night, when the sound was keeping everyone in the house awake, except for him, the lady of the house decided she had had enough. She headed to the laundry room to find what she needed, and went back to the bedroom where she proceeded to fix the snoring problem; or so she thought.

You have to appreciate the fact that this man had what would have been called a ski-jump nose. This was the air-intake valve; his mouth was the baffle that filtered the air out. Her thought process was to stop the air intake, and to do this she firmly placed a wooden clothes-pin on his nose.

Most humans who have their air intake blocked will resort to other methods of breathing, like opening up the output valve. Not this man. His continued attempt to use his air-intake valve, rather than open the baffle, was causing him some distress.

Within a few minutes it was clear that he was not about to breathe by any other way than his nose. The decision to remove the clothespin was made, and true to form he never missed a beat. The air-intake valve was as loud as ever and the baffle sputtered out the air, all as if the system had never been interrupted.

PARTNERS

Only he and I are in the box. All around us there are quiet murmurs, arena noise, and bawling calves. I know I need to stay focused and pay attention.

I can feel the anticipation and the calm coming from the man who sits astride me. I have been in this situation with him many times; a team made up of trust.

As always, he asks me to back tight into the far corner of the box. It is the perfect vantage point for us both. Out of the corner of my eye, I see the barrier being strung across the box in front of us. That's the sign that the technical part of this exercise is ready and waiting. With a slight pressure from his legs, he tells me that he too is ready.

I sense the nod of his head. It's time! I must hold back just a split second to make sure the barrier snaps open before we get to it.

We are out of the box and I am in charge of the chase. I feel the loop of the rope snake out past my shoulder and see it settling over the calf's head. The man is out of the saddle and on the ground; running down the rope while I keep it taut for him. I need to work the rope ever so slightly. I watch their every move. The man flips the calf, and gathers up two hind legs and a front one. With one fluent motion, the pigging string is tied with one wrap and a half-hitch. The calf lies still. I can relax, but only a little. Not until the man is back in the saddle and gives me the sign can I step forward.

The calf is released. The man coils up his rope and I move towards the gate at the end of the arena. There is talk from the announcer. I feel the slight tug of my mane. It is a quiet gesture of thanks from the one who has been my partner since he was a boy.

OLD COWBOY

He sits tall in the saddle with purpose and pride
His word, the firm handshake he offers
The voice is low and the gaze never wavers
Life as he knew it, taken in stride

His rope held casually, a tool of his trade
He leans on the saddle watching his world
Sunrise and sunset is the way he tells time
Life as he knew it, is what he has made

His hat and his chaps fit with a worn, tranquil grace
He has eyes that tell of wisdom, sorrow and love
The days in the saddle created his persona
Life as he knew it, shown by the lines on his face

His horse and saddle, used to play out his role
The one with the heart that is true
Giving to others a vision of hope
Life as he knew it, lives on in our soul

THE VALLEY

. . . She was twelve and in her mind she was a grown-up, spending the summer at her grandparents' ranch without her mom and dad. They would join her there before school started in the fall; until then she would spend all the time she could riding with her granddad . . .

It was late in the summer when Granddad announced at the dinner table that tomorrow would be a good day to check the fence line on the way to the valley. I kept my excitement to myself and went to gather up what I would need for a full day in the saddle.

We caught the horses just after daybreak. Saddled and ready they were given some grain to eat while we went to have the breakfast Grandma had cooked for us. While we ate, she made us a lunch to take along. We were on our way just as the sun peeked over the top of the barn.

The sun was not quite overhead when we came out of the trees to a small clearing. This is where Granddad said we would stop for lunch, as it was about an hour from our destination. He stopped, got off his horse, and squatted down to have a look at something on the ground. The grass had been trodden on and it was easy to see that an animal had passed through here.

"We'll turn back after we eat," Granddad said as he pointed out the big cat tracks in the soft dirt. "We can come another day."

I was devastated but tried very hard to mask the disappointment in my voice. "I would really like to go today, Granddad. The trucks will start to come tomorrow, and you will be busy shipping cattle until after I leave." In the end, we compromised. We would go to the valley to see the wild mares and their foals, and we would head back to the ranch to be home for dinner.

Granddad always took the trail to the rocks overlooking the valley. It was a safe vantage point to watch from without being seen. Today, he circled below the outcrop and we rode towards the far end of the valley. "Keep the wind at your face when you want to sneak up on something," is what he had always told me. The direction we were heading fit perfectly for his way of thinking; soon we would be on top of the rise where we could watch the horses below.

It was then that we felt the ground shaking. Our horses started snorting and sidestepping. The sound on the wind was a rumbling mixed with frantic whinnies from the animals in the valley.

Trying to sound braver than I was feeling, I quietly asked, "What's going on Granddad? Why are the horses running?" He never said a word as he motioned to me with his hand to keep quiet and stay put. He turned his horse to the top of the rise; at the same time, he pulled his rifle out of the scabbard. I was scared because I knew the gun was only ever to be used for a few things – shooting wild horses was not one of them.

I busied myself by pretending to calm my horse; patting his neck, and all the while watching Granddad from under the brim of my hat. As I thought of all the things that could be going on, I wanted to yell out to him, *Wait for me.* I knew better. This was serious.

I watched as Granddad stepped off his horse with his rifle in his hand, and dropped the reins. Slowly, he made his way to the edge of the ridge. Every move he made was like a slow-motion movie; never once doing anything that might call attention to his position. He leaned the rifle against a tree and from around his neck brought the field glasses up to his eyes. Somewhere inside my head I screamed, *What do you see?* Not a sound dared come from my lips.

Then I saw him move towards the rifle. He calmly picked it up and brought it to his shoulder. Without hesitation, he aimed down the valley towards the herd that I knew was there. My voice was locked inside me, silently willing him not to shoot the horses. I heard a shot and one more right after it. This time, my voice was real when I yelled out, "Granddad!" He lowered the rifle and turned towards me, once again motioning for me to stay put.

I sat motionless on my horse as I watched him put the rifle back where it belonged. He gathered up the reins and led his horse back down the rise to where I waited. When he reached me, he spoke softly: "We need to go down to the valley floor to make sure the mares and foals are okay. What we find might not be nice." As we made our way down the slope into the valley, Granddad talked quietly, explaining what he had seen and why he had fired two shots.

The big cat, a cougar, had been stalking the herd. That's what had spooked them to run. The whinnies we'd heard were the mares calling out to their babies to keep up. The cat had chosen a new foal as its prey. Its wobbly new legs couldn't keep up, so its mother had tried to keep herself between the foal and the cat. In hopes of being a warning, the first shot had been fired to scare the cougar off. When it had continued to circle the mare and foal, the second shot had ended the cat-and-mouse game. Granddad was pretty sure that the mare might be hurt, and he wanted to get as close as we could, to find out.

I had never been to the valley floor before and it seemed to take forever to get there. When we reached the bottom of the hill, we stopped. "Let the herd get used to us being here before we try to get to the mare."

I could see her. She stood with her head down. Her flanks were heaving and her shaking body glistened with sweat. She turned her head to nuzzle the little foal that was pinned to her side. Granddad was right. The mare had been hurt. The big cat had opened up her hip with its claws.

"What are we going to do, Granddad?" I whispered. I had been so mesmerized by the scene that I had not seen him untie his lariat from his saddle.

"I am going to try and rope her. I don't think she has much fight left in her. I think with your help we can get her and the foal back to the ranch where I can doctor her."

He wanted me to help! *Oh man*, I thought, *I am just a kid!* "What do you want me to do?" I asked. My hands were shaking and my voice didn't sound very convincing.

He smiled at me and told me what he expected. "When I get the rope on her, it is very important that you stay way back. I don't want you to get tangled in the rope if she decides she wants to fight or run. I will tell you when I want you to move in behind her and the foal. Just keep yourself the length of the rope away. Do you understand?"

I nodded and turned my horse towards the edge of the meadow where I would wait for Granddad's next set of instructions. He rode forward a bit and stopped. The mare looked up, but didn't move. Granddad waited and then moved towards her again. It wasn't until he was about ten feet from her that she started to move away, but then stopped and turned her head to look at the horse and rider. Granddad threw the loop and watched it make its mark. He quickly dallied the rope around the saddle horn and waited for the mare to explode. Wild horses are not known to like a rope on them, which is why Granddad had told me to stay way back.

She pulled back hard on the rope, her eyes white with fear, and her nostrils flared and blowing. Granddad's horse moved him into position and kept the rope tight. This was how it was for more than a half an hour; a waiting game to see who would break first. The mare finally took a few steps forward. The rope loosened and she dropped her head as if to say, *I'm done. You win.*

Granddad called to me to make my way around to the back of the mare. "Don't get between her and her baby; she needs to know it is safe beside her. I am going to start up the hill. She is going to fight the rope and is not going to want to be led away from the herd. Stay behind her and push her. You are my eyes back there. You have to tell me if you see something that could cause trouble for all of us. Understand?"

My voice didn't sound like me when I said, "Yes sir." So I nodded and he gave me a reassuring smile.

The mare struggled against the rope all the way to the top of the slope. After we reached the top of the rise, she seemed to straighten out and as long as she could see her foal, she moved along as best she could with the open wound on her hip.

This was going to be a long ride home and it would be dark by the time we got there. Grandma would be frantic with worry. What a story I was going to be able to share.

. . . *She leaned against the rocks, watching the mares and foals below. Her grandfather had brought her to this special place when she was a small child. Today she had come alone; just her and the sorrel horse that had been a gift from Granddad. She and the gangly colt had grown up together here on the ranch that was now home for both of them. The course of both of their lives had been changed on that day, ten years ago, when the big cat had come to the valley . . .*

MOONSET

Preferring to sleep
The sun goes down
Quiet but for the sound
Of the frogs chattering

A zone of tranquility
Stillness ricochets
Off the walls
And canyon floors

Left to darkness
The journey is slow
To above the rocks
And home for a few hours

Eventually descending
Over the ridge
The moon
Slipping silently

Through the trees
Out of view
From prying eyes
To sleep away the day

CPSIA information can be obtained at www.ICGtesting.com
Printed in the USA
LVOW07*1912021115

460796LV00003B/6/P